ANIMAL SUPERPOWERS

AMAZING PREDATORS

John Townsend

Raintree

Chicago, Illinois

www.capstonepub.com
Visit our website to find out more information about Heinemann-Raintree books.

To order:
☎ Phone 800-747-4992
💻 Visit www.capstonepub.com
    to browse our catalog and order online.

© 2013 Raintree
an imprint of Capstone Global Library, LLC
Chicago, Illinois

Edited by Rebecca Rissman, Dan Nunn,
  and Catherine Veitch
Designed by Joanna Hinton-Malivoire
Picture research by Mica Brancic
Production by Victoria Fitzgerald

Originated by Capstone Global Library
Printed and bound in China by CTPS

16 15 14 13 12
10 9 8 7 6 5 4 3 2 1

Library of Congress Cataloging-in-Publication Data
Townsend, John
Amazing predators / John Townsend.—1st ed.
p. cm.—(Animal superpowers)
Includes bibliographical references and index.
ISBN 978-1-4109-4749-9 (hb)
ISBN 978-1-4109-4756-7 (pb) 1. Predatory animals—Juvenile literature. I. Title.
  QL758.T69 2013
  591.5'3—dc23   2011041465

Acknowledgments
We would like to thank the following for permission to reproduce photographs: Alamy pp. 6 (© WaterFrame), 8 (© A & J Visage); Dr. Arthur Anker (UFC, Brazil) p. 12; FLPA p. 21 (Silvestris Fotoservice); Getty Images pp. 10 (Peter David), 16 (Digital Vision), 23 (National Geographic); Nature Picture Library pp. 9 (© Kim Taylor), 11 (© David Shale); Science Photo Library p. 7 (Pascal Goetgheluck); Shutterstock pp. 4 (© Christos Georghiou), 13 (© John A. Anderson), 14 (© Kjersti Joergensen), 15 (© Marjan Visser Photography), 17 (© bluecrayola), 18 (© Cathy Keifer), 19 (© Pierre-Yves Babelon), 20 (© Susan Flashman), 22 (© Art man), 24 (© Keith Levit), 25 (© Mogens Trolle), 26 (© Kletr), 27 (© Kletr), 29 (© Danomyte); p. 5 (Paul Whitehead).

Cover photograph of a crocodile reproduced with permission of Shutterstock (© Evlakhov Valeriy).

Every effort has been made to contact copyright holders of material reproduced in this book. Any omissions will be rectified in subsequent printings if notice is given to the publisher.

We would like to thank Michael Bright for his invaluable help in the preparation of this book.

Disclaimer
All the Internet addresses (URLs) given in this book were valid at the time of going to press. However, due to the dynamic nature of the Internet, some addresses may have changed, or sites may have changed or ceased to exist since publication. While the author and publisher regret any inconvenience this may cause readers, no responsibility for any such changes can be accepted by either the author or the publisher.

Some words are shown in bold, **like this**. You can find out what they mean by looking in the glossary.

Contents

Animals Can Be Supervillains!

Supervillains in stories have scary superpowers that can do harm. But did you know that some animals also have frightening skills? Read this book to find out which animals use superpowers to frighten their enemies.

Did You Know?
The tiny shocking pink dragon millipede has a secret weapon. It can give out a deadly gas.

Super Zap

Many animals with supervillain powers live in rivers and oceans. The electric eel can **stun** or kill **predators** with electric shocks. A 2-foot-long electric eel is the length of about 12 soccer balls in a row. It can zap 500 **volts**—enough to kill an adult human.

Did You Know?

Scientists use special nets to scoop electric eels up. Otherwise they would get a nasty shock!

Super Shoot

Did you know that some fish can shoot? The archerfish is an expert water shooter. It can fire from five feet away and hit its target with its first shot. The jet of water knocks any insect into the river, and the fish gulps it down.

Did You Know?

Archerfish can also leap from the water to snatch insects that come too close.

Super Trick

The anglerfish lives very deep down in the dark sea. It might look ugly, but the anglerfish attracts its **prey** by using a clever trick. To draw small fish toward its open mouth, it has a light on the end of a spine like a fishing pole. This hangs above its sharp teeth.

light

Super Strike

The pistol shrimp can make a noise so loud that it can kill! It has a giant claw that snaps shut and fires a super-hot bubble at **prey**. The bubble bursts louder than a blast from a jet. These "water bullets" can kill small fish.

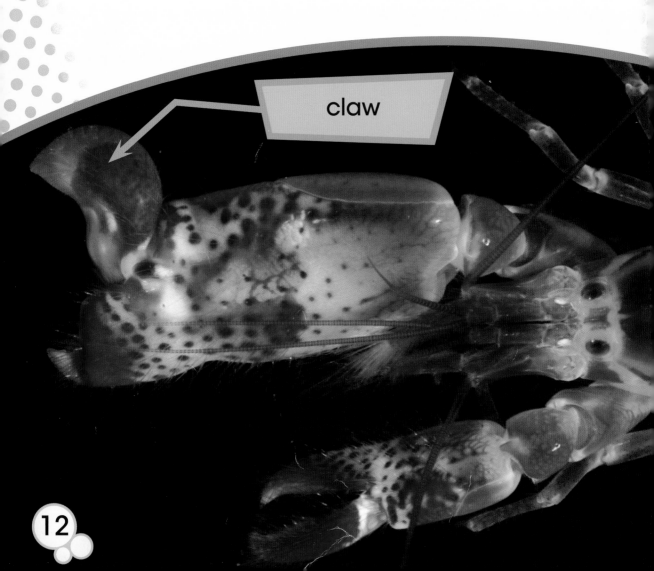

claw

front legs

Did You Know?

A mantis shrimp can thump its prey to death with its front legs, with the force and speed of a bullet.

Super Stun

Cuttlefish use amazing superpowers to catch their **prey**. As they swim, hover, or walk along the sea floor, they can change color to look like flashing lights. This **hypnotizes** other fish so that they cannot move. The cuttlefish can gulp them down.

Super Scary

Reptile predators use scary superpowers. The spitting cobra can shoot out deadly **venom** with perfect aim. This killer snake raises its head, spreads out its hood, and sprays blinding venom straight into the eyes of its **prey**. Ouch!

hood

Did You Know?

One bite from a king cobra can release enough venom to kill an elephant.

Super Tongue

Chameleons are **reptiles** with many superpowers. They can change color to scare away or hide from **predators**. They can also catch **prey** with their sticky tongues. A chameleon's tongue is longer than its body!

This chameleon has just changed color— one of its superpowers!

tongue

Super Snapper

The biggest **reptile** with amazing attacking powers is the super-strong crocodile. The Nile crocodile is a perfect killing machine. Its jaws are strong enough to crush some animals' skulls.

Did You Know?

This saltwater crocodile rolls its **prey** over and over underwater, to twist off chunks of meat small enough to swallow. This is called a death roll.

Super Drinker

Vampire bats in South America are **mammals** with supervillain powers. They drink blood! After dark, the bats fly from their caves. They can hear the heavy breathing of a sleeping animal and smell its blood from far away.

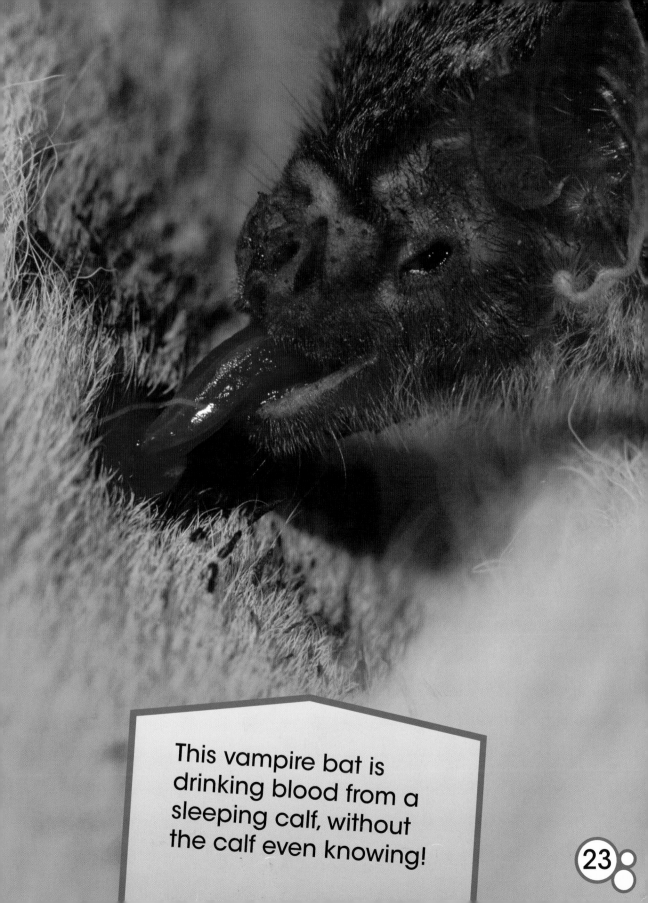

This vampire bat is drinking blood from a sleeping calf, without the calf even knowing!

Super Killer

The lion is known as the king of the beasts. Lions are expert hunters at all times of the day. They are especially good at hunting in the dark because of their excellent night **vision**.

Did You Know?

A lioness does most of the hunting. With super-strong jaws and teeth, she quickly kills with one bite to the neck.

Super Deadly

Of all the scary **predators**, the anopheles mosquito kills more humans than anything else on the planet. This tiny insect carries the deadly disease malaria. Each year, malaria kills more than one million people in Africa alone.

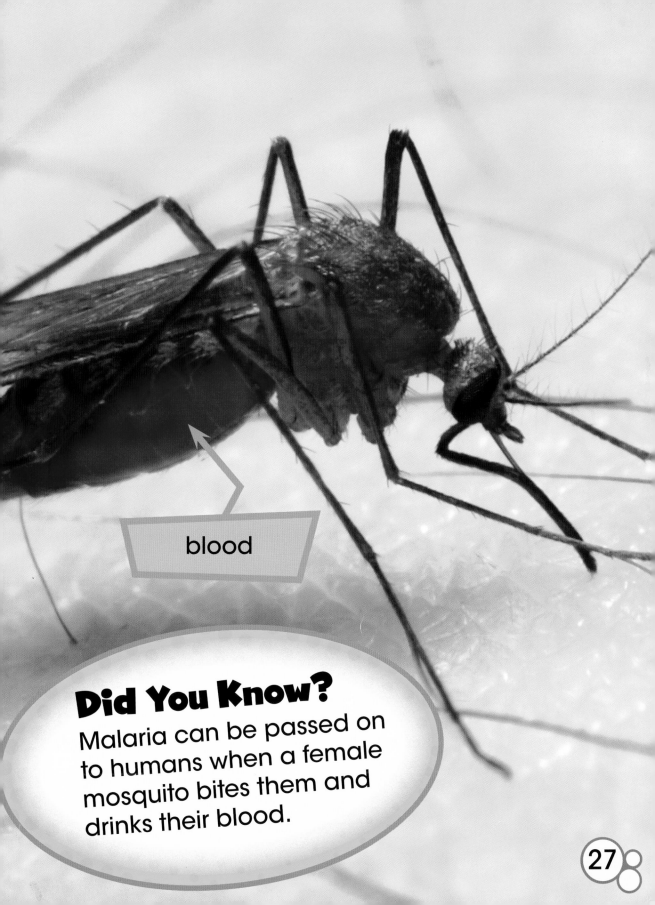

blood

Did You Know?

Malaria can be passed on to humans when a female mosquito bites them and drinks their blood.

Quiz: Spot the Supervillain!

Test your powers of observation and see if you can spot the supervillain. You can find the answers on page 32, if you are really stuck!

1. Which of these animals can give an electric shock?
a) an eel
b) a lion
c) a shrimp

2. Which of these animals can spit blinding **venom**?
a) a crocodile
b) a cobra
c) a millipede

3. Which of these animals can **stun** with sound?
a) a mosquito
b) a bat
c) a shrimp

4. Which of these animals can strike with a sticky tongue?
a) a chameleon
b) a cuttlefish
c) a lion

5. Which of these animals can catch **prey** with a light?
a) an archerfish
b) an anglerfish
c) an eel

Glossary

hypnotize put someone into a trance or sleep

mammal warm-blooded animal that makes milk for its young

predator animal that hunts other animals

prey animal that is hunted by other animals for food

reptile cold-blooded, air-breathing animal with scaly skin

stun knock unconscious

venom poison that is injected

vision eyesight

volt measure of electrical force

Find Out More

Books

Clarke, Catriona. *Reptiles* (Usborne Beginners). Tulsa, Okla.: EDC, 2009.

Gilpin, Daniel. *Record-Breaking Animals* (Record Breakers). New York: PowerKids, 2012.

Gilpin, Rebecca. *Dangerous Animals* (Usborne Beginners). Tulsa, Okla.: EDC, 2008.

Johnson, Jinny. *Amazing Animals* (Explorers). New York: Kingfisher, 2012.

Websites

animal.discovery.com/videos/fooled-by-nature-archer-fish.html
Visit this Website to watch an archerfish strike. (You may need to watch an advertisement before the archerfish video begins.)

www.yourdiscovery.com/video/natures-perfect-predators-cobra/
Visit this Website to watch a cobra spit venom. (You may need to watch an advertisement before the cobra video begins.)

Index

Answers: 1.a, 2.b, 3.c, 4.a, 5.b.